The Shuttlecock:

Recollections of an Evacuee 1939 - 1945

– BERNARD DRUMMOND –

An environmentally friendly book printed and bound in England by
www.printondemand-worldwide.com

Mixed Sources
Product group from well-managed
forests, and other controlled sources
www.fsc.org Cert no. TT-COC-002641
© 1996 Forest Stewardship Council

PEFC Certified
This product is
from sustainably
managed forests
and controlled
sources
www.pefc.org
PEFC/16-33-415

This book is made entirely of chain-of-custody materials

www.fast-print.net/store.php

Recollections of an Evacuee 1939 - 1945
Copyright © Bernard Drummond 2012

ISBN 978-178035-523-8

First published 2012 by
FASTPRINT PUBLISHING
Peterborough, England.
Printed by Printondemand-Worldwide

Preface

In the year of 1939, when the summer was nearing its end, the people of Great Britain were once more being warned to prepare for war.

In towns and cities, posters were appearing on hoardings and official bulletins were dropping through letterboxes with a variety of advice for the householder and parents.

The ARP, a section of the Civil Defence, were encouraging those with gardens to build Anderson shelters, and advising on how to tape windows for protection against flying glass. Massive air raids were feared and, because of this fear, the authorities were arranging for the evacuation of children under the age of fourteen to places of safety.

The *Oxford English Dictionary* describes evacuation as: *The removal of persons from an area of danger*. This may be an accurate description, but it cannot begin to describe the personal traumas that occurred as a result of the exodus of thousands of children (the majority unaccompanied by their parents) to the relative safety of the countryside.

Official figures state that of the one and a half million people evacuated, six hundred thousand were schoolchildren. Although some of their stories have been told, many retain bittersweet memories that will remain with them all of their lives. They were billeted in far-off villages, at a very important stage of their development, with varying experiences, some happy and some sad, but all with stories to tell about this important period of our history.

This is just one of those stories.

Introduction

On September the 3rd, 1939, I was eight years old and recovering from diphtheria. I was staying in the Princess Christian Home at Engelfield Green, which was a large house near Windsor. This was used by the Shaftesbury Society as a convalescent home, primarily for children from poor London households. The matron and staff in the home were kind and caring people, and I remember being very happy there.

Some memories of that time have remained vividly with me. The smell and feel of the rubber sheets that were in every bed, the communal showers and the strange black soap that we used. At night when we went to the dormitories, as we trooped up the stairs we passed an older boy who sat on the landing. He was in charge of a large wicker basket from which he gave us all a slice of bread and a piece of cheese for our supper. Apparently they didn't mind crumbs in the beds!

On that very historic day I was in the garden outside the house with the other children. We were waiting for our morning walk with one of the teachers when we were suddenly called into the large morning room. All the adults were there and appeared very serious as they sat us down in front of the large radio. We were told to be quiet as something very important was about to be broadcast In retrospect, what we then heard meant little to me, or to the other children at the time, but the effect that the broadcast had upon the matron, teachers and staff was quite evident, and we all knew that it was bad news.

What we had heard was the announcement by the then Prime Minister that our country had declared war upon Germany. I had no idea that Neville Chamberlain's solemn speech was to have such ramifications for the country as a whole or, more particularly, for children of my generation.

For me it was the beginning of an eventful six years during which I was evacuated and brought home no less than three times, like a little shuttlecock. First to Hertfordshire, then Devon and finally to Cornwall, until peace was declared in Europe, and I happily returned to London for the VJ Day celebrations in 1945.

Chapter 1

Sent To Safety

Hertfordshire

Within days of arriving home from Englefield Green, my mother had arranged for me to join other children who were to be evacuated to the safety of the countryside from our local school. This was a large and crumbling Victorian building which drew its pupils from the catchment area of shabby terraced houses and dwellings (sometimes grandly called mansions), and the many blocks of council-owned flats in North London.

It was the beginning of September 1939 and still warm, but over my jacket I was clad in my brother's hand-me-down raincoat, which was still a little large for me. Most of the other children seemed to be overdressed, but what they didn't wear they would have to carry. My mother was anxious to get to her part-time job at a local factory and was torn between staying with her lad and risking the wrath of her boss, or leaving me before the coach arrived.

Sept 1939, Aged 8.

The build-up of more and more children accompanied by their parents soon decided her, however. I seemed cheerful enough so, giving me a hug and a kiss, my mother hurried off and turned just once to wave goodbye, trusting me into the care of the teachers and volunteers who would shepherd us children during this great exodus.

★★★★★★

I had only known Tim vaguely before that first eventful day on the coach. The pavement seemed to be full of weeping children and distraught mothers, but I had clambered eagerly aboard to bag a window seat. As the coach gradually filled I was joined by Tim who, although rather taciturn at first, soon became as excited as me, chattering about the forthcoming adventure.

The first part of our journey was a relatively short ride through London's dusty streets to a large railway station where we would board the train that was waiting to take us to the safety of the countryside. The station was already teeming with hundreds of children, some animated and as excited as me and my new found friend, some quiet and tearful. But in common with each other we were all 'labelled' and every child carried the ubiquitous gas mask. As the morning wore on, more and more children filled the platforms and the sound of their chatter and the noise of the train's engine building up steam became almost deafening. Finally, we were all assembled, the signal came and Tim and I clambered aboard, unceremoniously pushing our way to the window seats.

We soon began to find that we had other things in common apart from an obvious love of comics. I had brought a selection of my favourite *Wizards* and *Rovers* and was quite happy to share them with Tim. In return, Tim gradually introduced me to some select language that made my hair curl.

"How do you spell that?" I constantly asked, but to no avail. And I was later to find out that Tim's superior 'wouldn't *you* like to know' look hid a profound ignorance of spelling!

We also discovered that we had elder brothers serving King and Country as soldiers, and naturally we proudly felt part of the national excitement.

Our homes were in identical adjoining blocks of flats, separated only by a manicured lawn protected by iron railings. These served to reinforce the 'Keep off the grass' signs. Asphalt grounds adjoined the buildings and, when they were not being used for the purpose of drying clothes, us children would play there, ignoring the 'Ball games are strictly forbidden' notices (but only when the caretaker wasn't looking!). There were several parks and grassy open spaces within easy walking distance. Twenty minutes away by trolleybus or tram there was always Hampstead Heath, the Bank Holiday venue for so many Londoners. Like many of our fellow travellers that day, we were totally unprepared for the vista of hedges, woods and rivers that suddenly began to fill the horizon. The game of counting horses and cattle soon became pointless, there were too many!

The train journey eventually came to an end and, after another lengthy wait followed by a headcount, we left the quaint rural station. Led by the adults in charge, we walked through the streets lined with gaping sightseers. Eventually we arrived at a large cobbled square surrounded by shops and stalls which was the heart of a small market town. It was also the local bus terminus, and there stood the coaches commissioned to take the little evacuees upon the final leg of their journey. After another roll-call the teachers distributed some welcome refreshments of sandwiches and drinks before they led us in crocodile fashion to queue once more, but this time at the pungent-smelling municipal toilets.

Soon we were off again, but now the route became narrow and winding, with little to see except the dark green hues of hedges and trees. Passing several little hamlets until eventually arriving at the little village where a small reception party was waiting. By now we were tired, travel-sick and very apprehensive. Pale-faced, we climbed down from the coach and slowly filed into the village hall. This small wooden building was filled with villagers and families from the surrounding parishes who had been patiently awaiting the arrival of the coach and its cargo of nervous children, to whom they were willing to give a temporary home.

With little ceremony, in company with the other children we were lined up to one side of the building and eventually singled out to be taken home by our new foster parents. The girls seemed to be chosen first, being thought of as generally cleaner and quieter than the boys, then the better-dressed boys. Sisters and brothers clung together, refusing to be parted, and were amongst the last to be found a foster home.

Tim and I had by now become quite inseparable. We sat on the floor trying to distance ourselves from the other evacuees and the chattering villagers. Arms folded and unsmiling, we had both had enough of this adventure. Tim had convinced me that by appearing grumpy and thoroughly unfriendly, there was a very good chance that no one would choose us. We would either have to be taken back to London or, at worst, to the little town where we had stopped; at least there were shops and a picture palace there!

We had reckoned, however, without Mrs Harris. This formidable woman and her husband Tom were only in their early fifties, but the hardness and early poverty of life working on the land had aged them prematurely. They had raised two sons who had both married young and were now both serving in the armed forces. In spite of the early struggle of their lives, Mr and Mrs Harris still had room in their home and hearts for more children. The two scowling and slightly scruffy boys held no terrors for Mrs 'H'. As she silently appraised the two of us she could probably remember her own lads as rebellious eight-year-olds, and could see nothing in our faces that a good scrub and a bit of supper wouldn't remedy.

So we found ourselves reluctantly traipsing along behind a large maternal figure that marched ahead of us, with our little bundles of possessions clutched in her big red hands. With our gas masks swinging from our shoulders, we gradually became amused by this quaint, pinafored figure that had taken charge of us, and cheekily mimicked her slightly bow-legged gait as we made our way along the lane.

The destination was a small end-of-terrace cottage; inside it was dark and cluttered with furniture. At the back of the cottages were brick-built outhouses from which came a faint smell of drains and would be introduced to us as the chemical toilet, which would become a major trauma for me. The stench of rotting vegetation emanated from a shallow drainage ditch that ran down from the elevated back garden.

We hardly had time to remove our jackets when Mr Harris arrived home from his day's work. He greeted us cheerfully in his broad country accent, and heartily shook hands with us both. And while Mrs Harris prepared the supper, he showed us around the buildings and extensive back garden. To our delight, we were introduced to the two independent cats, and then to the chickens, ducks and tame rabbits that we were soon to discover featured heavily in the diet of the household. Tim and I gazed longingly at the still-laden fruit trees and were allowed one small windfall each. ("We mustn't spoil our supper," said Mr Harris.)

There were dozens of articles that we began to discover, all foreign to children that were born and bred 'townies'. Water-butts (which we would one day discover had a more sinister use than simply collecting rainwater), scythes, shears, forks and spades, and a magnificent wheelbarrow that was earmarked for future escapades not remotely connected with gardening. Last, but certainly not least, we were shown the outdoor 'lavvy'. This establishment, that we had smelt earlier, came complete with bluebottles and ancient newspapers, and was something neither of us would ever get used to!

Mr Harris was short in stature, but immensely strong; he seemed to be amused by us, and he obviously enjoyed our company, taking great delight in unravelling the mysteries of country life to us. But inside the little cottage he became a quieter man, invariably sitting at the head of the kitchen table waiting for his meal, his eyes fixed upon some object in the backyard. He puzzled us boys by his silence, even though he had told the two of us soon after our first meeting, that, "Mrs Harris don't hear too good," and then adding, "it doesn't do to laugh too much."

We boys soon discovered the implied warning in this statement.

Her approaching deafness had made Mrs Harris frustrated and, at times, rather irritable. Laughter that she didn't share in, especially if it was in her proximity, was assumed to be directed at her, so all attempts at humour were to be treated with extreme caution, making mealtimes fraught with danger. Mr Harris and us boys had to be scrubbed, seated and silent before the meal was served. Even when Mrs Harris's back was turned, we soon discovered that she could detect the slightest movement of hand or lip with the aid of a strategically placed mirror that hung on the wall in her small pantry.

★★★★★★

It was during the first week in our foster home that we were made aware of the fact that whereas Mr Harris seemed to possess a great sense of humour, Mrs Harris apparently seemed to have none. The occasion was a Sunday lunchtime and we were seated at the spotless kitchen table staring out of the window, when Mr Harris asked quietly, and of no one in particular, "Be that thunder I can hear, or gunfire?"

We boys barely had time to consider this seemingly serious question when Mr Harris broke wind. It was an enormous fart that resulted in peals of hysterical laughter from Tim and me. Mrs Harris had heard nothing of her husband's involvement in this outrageous behaviour and proceeded to scold and then threaten us with the wet dishcloth. Meanwhile, seemingly oblivious to the mayhem that he had caused, Mr Harris carried on looking out of the window whilst slowly shaking his head in disapproval.

★★★★★★

"It was only a little stain," I complained. "I mean," I carried on, "the carpet soaked most of it up."

Tim didn't answer, he was too busy sulking, and besides, the bump on his head was throbbing and seemed to be growing larger by the minute. We slouched miserably along the country lane, heads down, with hands thrust deep into our pockets. I had never been struck in anger by an adult before, and although the slap had stung, I had been more surprised than hurt. Tim, on the other hand, was quite used to avoiding the wrath of his father and elder brothers, and could see a clip around the ear coming a mile off. Unlike me, he had moved his head quickly out of the path of Mrs Harris's swinging palm, but unfortunately he was still not used to the geography of the tiny kitchen and had made painful contact with a corner of the dresser, hence the throbbing head.

"It's that flipping lavatory," I grumbled, and Tim silently nodded his agreement. We both disliked the smelly outside closet and had become quite nervous about using it at dusk; it was primitive compared to the indoor lavatories that our own council flats boasted. Although we had soon got used to the pedestrian woodlice, it was the larger, faster-moving creatures that we imagined were lying in wait under the seat that had us worried.

It never occurred to either of us to put the blame on Mr Harris, we knew that he was only having one of his jokes last night. He had been sitting just outside the back door, as had been his custom for years past, filling his pipe for a last smoke before retiring. We had been sent out 'to do our business' on Mrs Harris's orders, before bedtime. Old Tom usually had a friendly word or jest to offer as we passed him, and last night he had advised us mischievously to, "Watch out for Old Jack!"

This casual reference to a legendary giant spider that he claimed to have seen previously lurking in the dark recesses of the smelly outdoor closet was enough to make both of us suddenly lose the desire to do any sort of 'business' right then. As a consequence, during the night we had both needed to use the large chamber pot that the practical Mrs Harris had placed beneath the bed when we had first arrived at the cottage.

The following morning, Mrs Harris called us down for breakfast and there was the usual pushing and shoving as we endeavoured to be the first to get dressed. This morning, however, there developed a full-scale pillow fight. It was never established exactly who knocked over the chamber pot; all we could do was watch horrified as the contents disappeared into the carpet. The two of us had only just arrived downstairs before the stain of our guilt began to appear on the kitchen ceiling. I couldn't take my eyes off the spreading, darkening evidence, and within seconds Mrs Harris was following the direction of my startled gaze.

If asked, we would probably have grudgingly admitted our guilt, and even the justification of Mrs Harris's screaming fit, but it was the lack of breakfast that really hurt! Under the circumstances, we had left the cottage rather hastily that morning, but Tim had managed to grab the satchel that usually contained our lunch and, much to our relief, we found that the familiar tin contained not only sandwiches, but cake also. This food was meant to keep us going until we arrived back from our lessons sometime in the early afternoon, but we were hungry now! We climbed over the first fence that we came to and settled down under the protection of a hedge to breakfast upon Mrs Harris's generosity, and soon began to feel much more predisposed towards her.

The school was about a mile away in the next village, but there was plenty of time on this beautiful September morning and there were still plenty of surprises along the hedgerow awaiting two young evacuees. Fortified by the sandwiches, Tim and me soon began to cheer up; thoughts of our former homes, the cosy council flats with their inside lavatories, were soon forgotten when we remembered the orchard. It wasn't exactly on the way to school, but we did have plenty of time. At this hour of the morning we might be able to do some scrumping in relative safety.

Cutting across the fields, and skirting the church and its spooky, decaying graveyard, we set off in what we hoped was the direction of forbidden fruit. The area was still pretty new to us, we had after all only been in the village for four weeks, but were still very surprised when we came upon a river. The water was wider here than at the village, where it ran beneath the old stone bridge; it was also quieter and, as the locals knew, much deeper. There was no footpath on either side of this stretch of river, running as it did through privately-owned land, just wonderful grassy banks sloping down to clumps of reeds inhabited by moorhens and amphibious creatures that splashed out of sight leaving only ripples on the water's surface as we ran noisily alongside. Some stretches of the bank were several feet higher than the water, but here and there it was possible to lay stretched out with faces only inches from the river, watching minnows beneath the surface and marvelling at the water boatmen seemingly walking upon the water.

I recall sitting on the bank, looking around trying to get my bearings, searching for some familiar landmark. Considering my rather limited vision, this wasn't easy (the measles that I had suffered from some four years earlier had left me quite short-sighted, a fact that so far had escaped the notice of adults) . I squinted back along the way that we had come.

"Can you see the road?" I asked Tim.

"Nope," said Tim, "but I think I can see the orchard."

The thought of the fruit-laden trees sent us boys whooping and galloping across the field on imaginary steeds, expertly avoiding cowpats and molehills. As we grew nearer, we soon realised that what Tim had mistaken for the bountiful orchard was in fact an ancient overgrown garden with the wreck of an old cottage in its centre. There were apple trees all right, but years of neglect had shrunk the quantity and size of the fruit. Nettles and brambles surrounded them and helped to keep the fruit out of reach. I nervously peered up into the branches of the fruit trees trying to detect the presence of wasps, because I had received a painful lesson on the morning after my arrival in Morchard.

We had been sent to watch the men of the village filling sandbags with which to fortify the village hall. Each of us had been given an apple by Mrs Harris, and as we began to eat, the fruit attracted the attention of several wasps. Tim, who seemed to be able to eat at twice the speed of me, had soon disposed of his apple, hurling the tiny core away. I was not going to be hurried by a few insects, however, and furtively hid my half-eaten apple behind my back, and soon discovered that that was not the way to deter persistent wasps! Mrs Harris had performed some magic with vinegar and soda that took away some of the painful effects of the stings, but from that time onwards I was wary of any flying insect that 'buzzed'.

In the meantime, Tim, who had no such inhibitions, was being practical and had found an old door amongst the debris of the building. Together we manhandled the door against the trunk of the most promising tree, and in an instant Tim had clambered up to the lowest branch and was soon high enough to reach the fruit. It was hardly worth the climb, but Tim was enjoying the adventure and with his shirt and pockets full of the stolen prizes, he returned triumphantly to the ground. Tim began to share out his booty, handing the smallest and speckliest fruit to me. Retracing our steps back to the river and sitting on its banks, we had soon eaten our fill.

"What about school?" I asked eventually.

"It's too late now," replied Tim.

Neither of us boys had any idea about the passage of time, but the sun was growing hot and apart from the birdsong, there was not a sound to be heard. Tim had already decided that he was having too much fun to be bothered by school. Being no stranger himself to playing truant, he easily persuaded me to come around to his way of thinking. The arguments were obvious; we were already late, and didn't know how to get there directly from the river, and even if we did retrace our steps to the village, we would still have a couple of miles to walk along the country road.

"By then it would be home time anyway," reasoned Tim.

He was referring to the fact that because the numerous evacuees had to share the tiny school, with its cramped classrooms and inadequate facilities, with the local children, the authorities had arrived at the solution of opening the school to the Londoners in the mornings, reserving the afternoons for the local children. Not surprisingly, all the children thought that this was an excellent scheme, using the time gained from onerous studies to making the most of the remaining summer weather. I must admit that I had not needed to struggle overmuch with my conscience. The glorious weather plus Tim's enthusiasm had decided me that this was not really truancy. So having arrived at this decision, we began to make the most of the day.

We had found a part of the river that was used as a cattle crossing when the water was low and, having discarded shirts, socks and shoes, splashed happily in the shallows vaguely trying to build a dam. Tim soon became bored with the effort of trying to find materials for the construction and began idly kicking at what we had managed to build so far. At my protestations, Tim began a new game, which was simply seeing how far he could project mouthfuls of water. Finding myself the main target, I happily reciprocated until inevitably falling headlong into the water whilst trying to take avoiding action. When Tim stopped laughing and I stopped moaning we wrung my pants and shorts as dry as we could and then laid them out to dry.

Whilst I sat on the bank in my shirt, miserably waiting for my shorts to dry, Tim wandered off, ostensibly in an effort to find a shortcut back to the main road. He found himself side-tracked by a hedge full of delicious blackberries, which went a long way to assuage the growing hunger pains. As he ate his way along the hedgerow, he was aware of the sound of children's voices coming towards him. Two fellow evacuees, a brother and a sister, were making their way across the field to a farm which had become their foster home. Tim was startled to see them because they were carrying satchels, and it was a near certainty that they were returning from the morning session at school. Scampering back down through the field and then along the riverbank, he breathlessly told me of his fears that it was time that we made our way back to Mrs Harris and the cottage.

Reluctantly donning my still-wet shorts, and thrusting my pants into my pocket, I joined Tim who had somehow managed to tread into a fairly new and very smelly cowpat. He decided that a wet shoe and sock was preferable to the disgusting mess that he now possessed, and proceeded to wash his foot in the river. Seeing how odd his feet now looked, he promptly stuck his other foot into the water, reasoning that it was, after all, the lesser of two evils, at least they matched.

With much trepidation we slowly squelched our way back to what we imagined, at best, would be an uncertain welcome. As we neared the village we stopped for a conference at which we decided that we would try to sneak into the back garden and carry on with the weeding of the vegetable plot. This was a task we had been given the previous day and so far had hardly touched. We hoped such a good deed might put us back in favour with the formidable Mrs Harris.

We had barely reached the garden when a familiar voice bellowed from the kitchen doorway, "Do you boys want any lunch today or not?" Dutifully we presented ourselves at the kitchen table, eyes downcast. "Wash!" demanded Mrs Harris over her shoulder. "And change those school clothes."

Unable to believe our luck, we dashed off to change and clean ourselves up. We had already noticed that the bedroom rug was pegged to the clothesline in the yard, having obviously been washed during the day, and prepared ourselves for another telling-off – but amazingly it never came!

What Tim and me did not know and would never find out was the reaction of Mrs Harris to the morning's events once she had had the time to calm down. There was, after all, no real damage done, her husband could easily whitewash the ceiling that weekend. She felt that the boys had already been sufficiently punished, especially Tim, whose head had made such a sickening contact with the dresser, which she had felt rather than heard. In truth, she felt a little sorry for us afterwards but was determined not to show it. We even got away with our absence from school that day. With two less children in a class the teachers felt it to be a reason for rejoicing rather than an investigation. Unfortunately, as far as us miscreants were concerned, it only made truancy a little easier for us the next time.

******

Life soon returned to normal in the little cottage. That weekend, we were allowed to help Mr Harris whitewash the kitchen ceiling, whilst Mrs Harris visited her sister who lived in a nearby market town. Unashamedly we made the most of her absence, whooping with laughter when Mr Harris once managed to step backwards off the stepladder into the bucket of whitewash. Us boys blamed each other for the accident but Mr Harris was able to see the funny side of the incident and cleaned up the mess with no fuss. This was simply one more gesture of friendship that endeared him to us boys. We enjoyed our day together with him more than any so far since we had left our family homes.

★★★★★★

Sundays had become a pain to Tim. From the beginning of our stay at the cottage, Mrs Harris had insisted that we should accompany her to morning service at the village church. I wasn't too upset at this ritual for I had, after all, been quite used to church services at the 'home' I had stayed in just before the outbreak of war. There had been a heavy emphasis on religious teaching, with prayers at mealtimes and a service every night before bedtime. Tim, on the other hand, was not used to organised religion, apart from the morning assembly at school. He fidgeted all through the Sunday services, grumbling and muttering to himself.

It was after the first Sunday, that we met David for the first time. David was the vicar's only son, a year older than Tim and me, with a very posh voice. Much to our envy, we discovered that David did not attend school, but was taught by his mother who had been a teacher before her marriage. David was drawn to us like a moth to a candle. He was fascinated by our knowledge of a world to which, as yet, he was a stranger. He had seldom been taken to the cinema, and the Saturday morning 'tuppenny rush', as described to him by Tim and me, sounded so exciting. He had never heard of *The Three Stooges*, *Roy Rogers* or any of the characters that filled the pages of our comics. Tim and I couldn't believe such ignorance, and first set about educating him by loaning him comics (that he had to smuggle into his bedroom to read).

Tim told David lurid stories of life in London peppered with oaths that continually had to be explained to him.

"What does 'crikey' and 'blimey' mean?" he would ask.

"Stop asking questions while I'm talking," Tim would respond, not knowing the answer himself.

David learned many things in our company that his mother would have been surprised at, and in return for this mild corruption, he shared many of his secret haunts with us.

The most interesting place that he took us to was also potentially the most dangerous; this was the weir. Until we met David, our interest in the river virtually ended where it ran under the village bridge and continued its course into the land belonging to the local squire. The only entry into this land, as far as we could see, was a solitary gate set in the high hedge that ran the length of the village leading to the church. David earned our respect by disclosing the whereabouts of a small and partly hidden gate that led directly from the churchyard into the squire's land.

One memorable Sunday afternoon, David led us boys through the gate. The plantation that ran either side of the drive leading to the squire's house afforded excellent cover to us three trespassers as we made our way down to the river.

It was far too risky to bathe in the waters that led into the weir, and quite apart from the signs that warned of the dangers, the very noise of the cascading water was enough to discourage us all. David, however, knew of a spot further down where the water was deep enough for swimming. He was well prepared, wearing swimming trunks beneath his shorts and had soon stripped off and was ready to show his new-found friends some skills that we did not possess. As David showed off, diving into the water then executing a splashing, overarm back to the bank, Tim and me had stripped to our underpants and were contemplating the depth of the river at the edge. Neither of us could swim, although Tim professed that he could 'in the baths'. I knew what he meant; the water was always clear in the indoor swimming baths of home, there were steps at the shallow end and you could practise the doggy paddle without getting out of your depth. Altogether more civilised than this stretch of river with its clinging reeds and murky unknown pools.

Today, we were content to watch for a while. But as David became tired of swimming alone, he discovered that we had also become bored and had wandered off to a nearby hedge to look for old birds' nests. David had not managed to smuggle a towel out of the vicarage and improvising with handfuls of grass and dock leaves, he had hurriedly dressed and ran to join us. He was feeling the effects of the cold water and began shivering slightly.

Unknown to David and me, that morning Tim had pocketed a box of safety matches that he had found lying around in the church. Producing them, he suggested lighting a small fire by which David could warm himself. We all thought this an excellent idea and set about forming a pyramid of dry grass and dead twigs, which abounded in the area. Only after the fire was well and truly alight did we realise that we had made the fire a little too close to the hedge. We watched in horror as the flames caught and raced along the hedge.

We quickly ran for the shelter of the plantation and sneaked red-faced back into the churchyard. The tell-tale smoke was rising thickly as us boys wandered nonchalantly back to the cottage. Fortunately, many of the villagers, including Mr and Mrs Harris, were still sleeping off the effects of their Sunday lunch, so this time there were no witnesses to connect the fire to the evacuees. Tim had sworn David to secrecy, craftily warning him of the terrors of police interrogation. As an afterthought, he thrust the matches into David's pocket, asking him to replace them in the church, thereby ensuring the guilty silence of the vicar's son.

★★★★★★

One of the family cats was heavily pregnant and Tim and me awaited the forthcoming event with great anticipation. The cats were never allowed into the cottage and were fed in the yard, sleeping in the tool shed upon piles of old sacks. Every morning, before leaving for school, we would peep through the grimy shed window to see if the kittens had arrived. When the magic day finally came, we could hear the tiny creatures mewing as we approached the shed, and excitedly ran to tell Mr Harris.

He warned us to keep away from the cat and its litter at first, but within a day or so he brought out two tiny bundles of fur for us to hold. The initial wonder soon gave way to pure joy as we both gently fondled the still-shaking kittens. I must confess that I was overcome with emotion. Tim was used to my occasional soft ways by now, but was embarrassed to find that he too was blushing with happiness as he held the small warm body in his hands.

The following day after school, we had run to the vicarage to fetch David so that he could see and perhaps even hold one of the kittens as a special treat. Almost creeping up the path, we slowly opened the shed door. The quietness of the shed surprised us at first, and the sole occupant, the kitten's mother, was fast asleep on her pile of old sacks. The three of us searched everywhere, but there was not a kitten to be seen.

"Perhaps they have been given away," ventured David.

We were soon to discover that the truth was far more horrible. The still little carcasses were at that very moment only a few feet away from us, bundled into an old potato sack suspended in the half-full water-butt where they had been put to drown.

Later that day, us boys, thoroughly puzzled by the kittens' disappearance, were to find that all our attempts to raise the matter were evaded by Mr Harris answering, "Not now boys," and the usual, "Be quiet!" from Mrs Harris.

Tim and I were to discover the grim reality of the situation that night from our bedroom window, as we watched Mr Harris go to the water-butt and retrieve the sack with its mysterious contents. Water gushed from the sack and left a trail behind him as he disappeared out of sight to the far end of the garden. Peering into the gathering gloom, we began to hear the sound of digging, and as the spade struck stony ground the awful truth slowly began to dawn upon us. We spoke about our suspicions in whispers, and as I tried to sleep, I began for the first time to feel really homesick.

The next day Tim, in his artful way, again raised the subject of the mysterious disappearance of the kittens with Mrs Harris.

"They are all gone," she snapped, "and that's the end of it!"

Tim was all for investigating the corner of the garden where the sounds of digging had come from the previous night, becoming excited and worked up at the prospect. I was, however, fearful of what we might find and would not hear of it. The death of the kittens was something that I was gradually coming to terms with; that was bad enough, but the thought that kindly Mr Harris had killed them, was almost too much to bear. The world, that day, seemed a gloomy place, and my sadness seemed to affect Tim, calming him down.

Resuming the investigation of the contents of our snack box, we made our way again to school.

★★★★★★

Soon after the evacuees had arrived from London some of the parents from our former school had arranged to visit their children. This they did by hiring a coach that began to come to the village on a Sunday. On one of these visits Tim's father and mother came to see him. I found out much later that Mrs Harris had written to them, apparently because she was finding it a little hard looking after two young boys. (Years later it did occur to me that Mrs Harris may have found Tim a bit of a handful and, although he had become my friend, I had to admit that he was inclined to be rather cheeky to adults, and I believed also that he did help himself from the larder on occasions, and Mrs Harris had caught him in the act.)

Much to my pleasure and surprise, I was told to accompany Mr Harris on this particular day, as he had some work to catch up on. The farmer that he worked for had lost some of his farmhands to the war effort. It was an interesting but tiring day watching Mr Harris carrying out his tasks of hedging and ditching, helping when I could by fetching and carrying. Old Tom was so friendly that day; we had shared our lunch together, and as usual he had kept me fascinated with a non-stop lesson on the ways of the countryside and the creatures that populate it. It was almost like old times, but not quite, not without my friend. I would make it up to Tim, I promised myself, by telling him every detail. As we finally began to walk home, I thought to broach the subject uppermost on my mind. Patiently, and with a certain sadness, Mr Harris slowly broke the news to me that Tim had left for good that day.

★★★★★★

During those first warm weeks of autumn that I had shared with Tim, we had forged a friendship that with the exception of David, had unconsciously excluded our fellow evacuees. It was only after Tim's departure that I realised how few children I was on first name terms with. Those that were not related to each other had formed friendships of their own and I found myself increasingly isolated at school. I was cruelly taunted by the older children and soon learnt not to react to the cries of, "Where's your friend Tim now?'" as I hurried home after classes were finished for the day. At the beginning, I called at the vicarage every day on my way home, hoping to see David, but each time I was sent away with different excuses until I gave up calling altogether.

★★★★★★

The weeks dragged by until I received a letter from my mother. At last she was coming to visit. Soon after Tim's departure, I had written to my mother begging to be taken home. As far as I was concerned the adventure was over and I had poured out my unhappiness on page after page. It was an unusually long letter for me. What I did not realise was that Mrs Harris had also written to my parents, setting out briefly the events of the past few weeks and the effect that they seemed to have on me. It was this message, rather than my own, to which my mother responded.

Sunday seemed to take forever to come but eventually I was there at the roadside waiting expectantly with the other children for the coach from London to arrive. As its occupants alighted from the coach, I was caught up in the excitement amongst the excited cries and laughter from the crowd. There was my mother at last, and much to my amazement, so was my brother John. I was pleased to see him, of course, but it did rather spoil my plans. John was eight years my senior, very tall and looking every inch a grown-up in his long trousers and tweed jacket. I had planned to spend the day persuading my mother to take me home, but the presence of my older sibling was going to make this difficult.

As we walked towards the cottage, I chattered excitedly to my mother and brother, pointing out all the now familiar haunts. I knew that all my intentions to appear sad and homesick were being undone by the natural happiness that I felt from being with my family again. But by the time they reached the cottage, I had collected my thoughts and remembered my plans.

Mrs Harris had prepared some lunch and invited them into the parlour. By removing the dustsheets that normally shrouded the furniture and ornaments, the room was transformed into a picture of cosy rural charm. She had performed the same magical trick upon herself, suddenly all smiles and generosity, even laughing at her husband's rustic humour! I flinched at the first pat on my head, and cringed when I heard her praising me. I became increasingly dismayed as I saw how impressed my mother was with this 'kindly soul', knowing in my heart that she wouldn't believe what an old battleaxe Mrs Harris could be. I couldn't wait for them to use the lavatory, even the recently applied coat of whitewash in honour of my mother's visit wouldn't hide the smell. With any luck 'Old Jack' or some other revolting insect might fall on her when she did eventually 'go'!

There was no denying it, Mrs Harris was a brilliant cook; her savoury pastries and fruit tarts were a revelation. I knew my brother and even my own mother would be extremely impressed with the fare provided for them. The day was becoming a complete disaster, and when Tom Harris had accompanied them on a gentle stroll after lunch, I realised that this last chance to exert some emotional blackmail upon my mother would be denied to me. The Harris's hospitality was genuine enough, as was their willingness to carry on providing a safe haven for me. As I tearfully waved goodbye to my family, I was well aware that as well as the homemade apple pie that my mother had been given, she was also taking with her the satisfaction that her youngest son was in good hands. Watching my mother wave cheerfully from the departing coach, I felt my unhappiness deepen.

★★★★★★

The fact that the mellow autumn had run its course was lost on me. I wasn't really aware of all the obvious signs in the countryside that the seasons were changing. The piles of fallen leaves that I now kicked my way through were beginning to show signs of decay and the hedgerows were bright with inedible berries. Winter was on its way and, as the weeks passed, life began to get a little easier for me at school. I began to make new friends and gradually found that I ceased to be the target for the taunts and jibes that had made my life such a misery since the departure of Tim.

It must have been early in December in that first year as an evacuee. I awoke that morning and knew that something strange had occurred. It all seemed to be so quiet. I usually awoke these mornings to the sound of Mr Harris bustling around below my bedroom window, chopping firewood to stoke the kitchen stove with before he left for work. But that morning there was a stillness and, as I went to the window, a magical sight greeted me. I rubbed away the frosted condensation from the panes of glass to discover that the back garden had disappeared under a blanket of snow. I rushed to the small window at the front of the cottage that looked out at the village, and was stunned by the beautiful transformation that I saw.

As yet, the roads and surrounding countryside were unspoilt, but I couldn't wait to dash out and be the first to plant my feet in its pristine surface. Although there must have been winters in my childhood before this when snow would have fallen, it would have soon thawed and turned to slush in the metropolis of London where I was born. This was something different, however.

★★★★★★

As the autumn had turned to winter, Mrs Harris had started dressing me in warmer clothes in which she had once dressed her own boys. Both of these lads had become men and were now wearing khaki, serving in the armed forces and, although I had never met them, they smiled down at me from their photographs that adorned the kitchen walls. These homespun woollen jumpers and leggings were obviously several sizes too big, but they were tucked and altered, and were a welcome alternative to the thin city clothes in which I had arrived. In particular, I remember a large woollen balaclava helmet that enveloped my head like a tea cosy on a teapot. The aperture that you were supposed to look through always seemed to be nearer my mouth than my eyes, but it did keep my ears warm!

Suitably fed and dressed, I pulled on the small pair of wellingtons that had been borrowed from a neighbour and, setting off for school that day to walk the one and a half miles to Waterdown, I joined up with other children who were also evacuees. And much to my relief they were also overdressed and looked just as ridiculous as I felt. By now the snow was falling steadily again, and as we trooped into the small school playground a barrage of snowballs and abuse greeted us. We were used to the abuse from the local children and were quite capable of returning it. I was singled out for most of the hilarity that ensued, as the local yokels pointed at my wellingtons, shouting, "He's wearing girl's wellies." I suppose that the colour, which was a sort of pink, was a bit of a giveaway!

It was hard to concentrate on the lessons that morning, as the snow continued to fall and the wind began to blow. After a couple of hours we were sent home, and I recall that walk back to Morchard, through a blizzard and gathering snow drifts that hid the ditches along the roadside. I managed to fall into one rather deep ditch, of course, and was completely immersed until I managed to scramble out. That scary experience helped me to view snow in a way that was neither beautiful nor 'smooth and crisp and even'.

As I said, this was not like the snow that fell in London, which melted and turned to slush the minute it hit the pavement. This snow was cleaner and seemed thicker somehow. When the winds blew it into huge drifts down the country lanes, it was so new and exciting. There were frozen ponds to slide on and occasional walks with old Tom through the hedgerows, now denuded of their leaves, displaying the remains of birds' nests. Then through the meadows and fields, now thick with frost that crunched beneath our feet, where hopefully we would find badger or fox tracks to follow. Somehow, this all helped to push the ever present desire for home a little further down my list of priorities.

★★★★★★

When Christmas came that year it was certainly different. It was the first one I had experienced away from my home and family, and one that I would remember for the rest of my life. The little cottage was full of the wonderful smells of Mrs Harris's cooking, days before the holiday. Not only did we collect our own holly and mistletoe, but there was also a freshly-cut Christmas tree that Tom Harris brought home. This was greeted with delight from me, but a torrent of abuse from Mrs Harris. It was 'too big', 'would make too much mess', he (her husband) was being 'too childish', and furthermore she 'wouldn't have it in the house!' Tom said not a word, but carried it around to the back of the shed and there, with a little help from me, proceeded to pot-up the tree in an old bucket. He then put it down outside the back door of the cottage and with a wink he nudged me with his elbow, whispering, "We'll see."

One image of that Christmas morning of 1939 that would always stay in my memory was the transformation of the cottage when I came down for breakfast. The parlour was open and a fire burning away in the grate. The room had been dressed and decorated with holly and mistletoe and, amazingly, there in the corner was the tree. Adorned with cotton wool and some ancient tinsel it looked magnificent. Even the redoubtable Mrs Harris had to laugh at the look of surprise on my face.

★★★★★★

The New Year came and the weeks passed by slowly as they do when you are bored and homesick. One day I arrived at the cottage after school and was surprised to find that Mrs Harris had received a letter from my mother. The woman made me sit down, and then gave me the news that I was going to be sent home. In spite of all the letters that I had written to my mother, pleading to be brought home, this news when it came was a great surprise. I had been treated very well really, and later would come to miss Tom Harris, a kind and friendly man. Even the strict Mrs Harris had fed and cared for me as well as any parent could.

I was not about to question what had caused the change of heart that led to my return home. I was still too young to realise that it was the time of the so-called 'phoney war'. Many children had returned from that first hurried evacuation as the immediate fears of most parents had passed. Although the war in Europe was going badly, it was still hundreds of miles away and the bombing raids had, so far, failed to materialise. Children returned to their former schools and familiar haunts, ignorant of the fierce fighting that was going on in France and Belgium.

But the reversals that eventually led to the defeat of the allied armies and the catastrophe of Dunkirk inevitably brought the war nearer to home.

1941, Aged 10-11.

Chapter Two
The Blitz Begins
Devonshire

By the summer of 1940 the Battle of Britain was being waged and the residents of the capital were being bombed in earnest. The air raids intensified at night and it was a time of great excitement to my friends and me, as we became sky watchers. During the daytime, the best vantage point for watching all the activity was from the top balconies of the many blocks of flats in London. In my case, my own block of flats faced north, and when a heavy raid was in progress in the south, there was very little to see. The solution was to run around to the companion building that faced south. Although the targeted City and Docklands were many miles away, the exploding flak was clearly visible in the sky. Unfortunately, the adults, and in particular the Air Raid Wardens, were born spoilsports and seldom allowed the children to watch these pyrotechnics for long. In theory, once the air raid sirens had sounded, unauthorised civilians had no business out on the streets.

The air raids at night were a completely different experience. The noise of the enemy aircraft droning overhead, the cacophony of anti-aircraft fire and exploding bombs, kept most people in their shelters. My family and me didn't have far to go to our own shelter because we lived on the ground floor. The next-door flat had been emptied and then converted into a shelter for the use of families in that particular block. As the 'all clear' siren finished, we would emerge to find streets sometimes lit by fires that the bombers had left in their wake. Only the mornings would reveal the full extent of the damage that had been done the night before.

For me and the few boys that I was now friends with, it was a time for exploring and shrapnel collecting. This bizarre activity was so popular amongst children in the towns that were being bombed that it resulted in them having tins full of the jagged remnants of exploded shells.

A more dangerous, but infinitely more attractive, pursuit was the investigation of bombsites. Children travelled far afield for the chance to clamber over the remains of someone's former home, playing through the roofless, empty rooms. Not only did we run the risk of serious injury, but also of detection by the various uniformed authorities. Police, Civil Defence and firemen all posed the same threat to scruffy little truants caught trespassing.

★★★★★★

In the autumn of 1940, the bombing became heavier and more widespread. My mother once more decided to evacuate her son to the safety of the countryside. So, in the company of hundreds of other children, I found myself once more staring out of the grimy windows of a train as it steamed west.

The journey was longer than any I had previously experienced, and my abiding memory would always be of the changing colours of the earth in the fields, eventually becoming a rich, dark red as our train travelled further west. When we finally arrived at our destination, it was to the sound of the guard crying out to the arrivals, "Crediton, Crediton Station!" and we clambered down from the train into the clamour of noise on the platform.

I was by now a much bolder child than when I was first evacuated, and asked a smiling lady (who from her official armband appeared to be one of the welcoming committee), "Where are we please, Miss?"

I was greeted with the response, "Why, my lovely, you be in glorious Devon, of course!"

Her answer and her smiling face filled me, and my travelling companions, full of hope that here indeed was the land of milk and honey. Thus encouraged, we boarded the coaches and set off into the countryside. This meant another village, another church hall reeking of paraffin alongside the rotting produce of the last harvest festival.

★★★★★★

During the long journey from London, I had befriended an older boy who was accompanied by his two young sisters. Bob was thirteen and a half and was a big lad for his age. He had confided in me that he had only agreed to the trip to keep an eye on his sisters. His father had given him his solemn word that as soon as he reached his fourteenth birthday he could return home. Bob had his future all planned out, starting with his eagerly awaited job with his dad as an apprentice in 'the print' until he was old enough to join his brothers in the army, where he'd learn how to 'cut the enemies throats!' Bob managed to sound thoroughly bloodthirsty, in spite of the fact that he, like me, was still clad in short trousers. The pronounced squint in one of his eyes gave him a slightly sinister air, and I must admit that I was a willing and receptive audience.

Bob's sisters were pretty and well-dressed, but they were not to be parted from their big brother, as successive villagers were to discover. Not only that, Bob had decided that I was also in need of his care and protection, and solemnly informed the billeting officer that the four of us could not be separated.

It was late in the day before a suitable home was found for the four of us, but we eventually found ourselves walking through the gates of what we presumed to be a farmyard. However, Mr and Mrs Bryant were not farmers, even though they did own a large house with an equally large and rambling garden. They also owned several acres of ground, which us children were to discover was rented by a local farmer. A hedge, with several well-used pathways cut through it, separated the house and garden from the fields, which appeared to have been recently harvested for grain.

Bob and I couldn't wait to explore this fascinating new home and surrounding grounds, but supper came first, and with it the introduction to the pre-meal routine that we would have to endure before we were ever allowed to sit down to eat. Us children soon discovered that Mr and Mrs Bryant were strict disciplinarians. Faces, hands and knees were inspected for dirt, hair had to be combed, and in the case of the girls tied back with ribbons, before we were allowed into the dining room.

Mrs Bryant was a nervy woman in her late thirties. Always active, she seemed to hop from place to place just like the sparrows that frequented the yard. Not surprisingly, us children quickly christened her 'Twitters'. Severe in dress and manner, her appearance was personified by her hair, which was always drawn back into the tightest of buns. Cleanliness was her major obsession, and meals would often go cold due to one of us unfortunate children being sent back to the bathroom, time after time, to remove some imaginary speck of dirt from hands or ears.

Mr Bryant always took his meals seated by a huge black stove in the kitchen. It was obvious from the very first day that this sullen and watchful man was someone to be feared. The only time we could ever relax properly was when he had gone to work. Mr Bryant seemed to earn his living by delivering produce from the local farms to the nearest market town and the small shops in the surrounding villages. His car, which he used for this purpose, was a revelation to me, but the fact that it soon became my job to clean and polish it, eventually made me come to hate the sight of it. Of course, Bob knew all about motor vehicles; his uncle drove a van for the very newspaper firm that one day would employ Bob. He had soon shown, however, that although he knew the theory of nearly everything, he was pretty useless at the practical side of things, thereby lumbering me with cleaning the car.

★★★★★★

I soon found that autumn in the Devonshire countryside was little different to autumn in Hertfordshire. I had yet to discover a river that compared with the one back at the Hertfordshire village that held so many memories for me, but there were other attractions. Nearby were two large woods and Bob had stumbled upon a deserted quarry on one of his lone forays.

The village school was similar to the one that I remembered in Hertfordshire, but with bigger classrooms and large enough to accommodate both local children and the small number of evacuees. It was only a five-minute walk away from our new home and, although at first we welcomed the shortness of the journey, it gave little scope for exploring on the way to and from lessons.

Tuesdays and Fridays, weather permitting, we were taken on long rambling walks by the old headmaster, who had been brought out of retirement to replace the teachers who were away helping the war effort. The walks were intended to teach the children something of the flora and fauna at first-hand. It was a good intention but, in reality, what always seemed to happen after a mile or two, was the discovery of a small copse, or even a haystack, where our leader would take a little rest.

Seated around him, us children would listen attentively as he began a lecture on an aspect of nature, which would then lead him into reminiscing over his life in the teaching profession or remembering some childhood anecdote. We soon learnt to listen quietly and patiently, for within ten minutes of starting his lecture, he would drift off to sleep, giving the bolder children the opportunity to sneak off and really explore nature.

★★★★★★

I would never forget my first, most humiliating experience. Before the cold weather really began, Mrs Bryant insisted that we had our twice-weekly bath outside the back door. This was taken in a large hipbath, with little privacy afforded for the bather. I was last in the pecking order behind the girls and then Bob. On this particular day, Mrs Bryant refreshed the water for me before setting off on a visit to her friend who lived locally. I had undressed quickly and had got into the water whilst it retained some vestige of heat, leaving my clothes on the chair. I didn't notice Bob removing them and was only alerted to the fact that something was going on by the laughter of the girls.

They began to run around the bath, giggling at my discomfort, waving my shirt and shorts like trophies, eventually draping them on some nearby fruit bushes, but well out of my reach. I sat in the old hip bath watching the goose-pimples begin to form on my arms; the water was quite cold by now and although the weather was still fine, there was the slightest hint of a breeze beginning to stir the trees. I guessed that my tormentors were hiding somewhere waiting for me to make a dash for my clothes. But because of my short-sightedness, I lacked the confidence to leave what little privacy the bath afforded me. Mrs Bryant eventually returned from her visit, but instead of giving me the sympathy I might have expected, she reprimanded me for being so stupid.

"Who do you think wants to look at you, you skinny thing?" she scolded.

I didn't answer, as I always had problems with questions like that.

★★★★★★

The village was quite large and its church, to which the girls and I accompanied Mrs Bryant every Sunday, boasted a considerable choir. Bob had become quite friendly with Mr Bryant, to the extent that he was never required to attend church with the rest of the children. Instead, he spent his Sundays with the older man out in the surrounding countryside mole catching and rabbiting.

I had a good treble voice and soon found myself drafted into the children's section of the choir, which I enjoyed tremendously. Strangely enough it was during choir practice that my myopia was first noticed. A trip to an optician in Crediton was arranged, and after the sight test I eventually received my first pair of spectacles. Naturally I hated the thought of wearing them, knowing full well that I would become another 'four eyes' to be made fun of, but the transformation in my vision was astonishing, literally changing my view of the world overnight. Many years later, I would discover that the vicar had paid for the sight test and the subsequent spectacles, an act of kindness for which I never had the opportunity to thank him.

★★★★★★

As remote as the village seemed, we were never completely isolated from the war, and two events took place over the winter months that brought a little excitement into our lives. The first was the appearance one morning of a barrage balloon, drifting over the fields towards the village. Where it had come from, nobody knew, but a posse of uniformed men and women were pursuing it, arriving in a convoy of camouflaged vehicles. The great silver balloon eventually settled slowly in the grounds of the vicarage much to the delight of the villagers and the disgust of the army. The vicarage was well protected by a high brick wall and by the time the recovery team arrived, the vicar and his stalwart verger were manning the only gate to it.

The lawns that spread in front of the vicarage were a great source of pride to the present vicar and had taken scores of years of careful gardening by the previous residents to arrive at their present immaculate condition. Now there was this huge nylon envelope of balloon, trailing yards of ropes, settled in the middle of the vicar's pride and joy, and he had no intention of allowing the huge army vehicles with their heavy-booted occupants anywhere near it.

News of the stand-off soon spread, and gradually people drifted in from the surrounding hamlets and farms to watch the fun. There followed hours of speculation and great excitement among the children and the villagers. In the meantime, however, I was solemnly informing every soldier who would listen to me that my eldest brother Bill was also in the army and came from

London – did they possibly know him? Much to my disappointment there was no spark of recognition from any of them, although one helpful soldier suggested that I should ask the little group of uniformed women if they had any news of Willy from London. The raucous laughter that followed made me abandon this idea, and later when I told Bob of this strange behaviour, my friend offered the opinion that it was the general secrecy of the army that made them appear so unhelpful.

Negotiations with the vicar must have eventually been successful because the balloon was deflated and carried away with no apparent damage to the vicarage and its grounds but with added respect for the status of both the vicar and the verger in the little community.

★★★★★★

A mile or so from the village was a large wood in which there was considerable tree felling taking place. Mr Bryant had constructed a cart and the girls and me had to visit the site for the purpose of collecting firewood. The large chips of wood that were made by the axe before the trees were sawn down made excellent firewood and us children would fill up the cart easily. We had been expressly forbidden to go near the quarry without an adult to accompany us, but unfortunately, neither Bob nor Mr Bryant could ever be persuaded to go there with us. So it was that one day with the girls, we decided to take a little detour just to look at what all the mystery was about.

A small copse stood at the edge of the quarry and the site itself was surrounded by decaying fences, tangles of barbed wire and brambles, and lots of 'DANGER –

KEEP OUT!' signs that were a sure invitation to any curious child. There were several well-trod paths that led through the trees to the quarry and we took one of the muddy and rutted tracks to the abandoned workings. It was all a bit disappointing. Immobile and rusting trucks stood on rails that disappeared into the undergrowth that had grown all around and halfway down the quarry face. The remains of a winch house had an oil-soaked space on the floor where I had guessed there had once stood a motor, and a frayed and twisted cable led from the building to the edge of the now quiet quarry. At the bottom lay a dark and uninviting pool of water; which none of us were brave enough to venture down to. A strange, sweet smell seemed to pervade the quarry that I was to discover many years later was the smell of cordite. We hurried from this place of decay with a shudder, and our curiosity completely satisfied.

The adventure did not pass without consequence after all, though. Molly couldn't resist telling her brother and when Bob tackled me about the trip, he was overheard by Mrs Bryant, who then took great pleasure in telling Mr Bryant. The punishment that followed was not of a physical nature, but there followed several early nights to bed, during which dearly-loved radio programmes were missed. The only consolation for me was that Molly and Joan also received the same sentence.

★★★★★★

The months passed until the advent of spring and Bob became more and more excited as his fourteenth birthday approached. The girls were also happy because their mother was coming to see them, even though she was taking Bob back with her. I remembered the visit well, especially seeing the girls ecstatic at seeing their mother again and then Bob's appearance in his first pair of long trousers that his thoughtful mother had brought with her.

There was also the inevitable change in Mr and Mrs Bryant's behaviour during their guest's stay, which reminded me of when my own mother visited me in Hertfordshire, and Mrs Harris's false geniality. I observed them from the fringe, marvelling at their joviality and kindness. Although not invited to share in it, I did not begrudge Bob and his sisters their happiness. There were, after all, the benefits of the little treats and improved food and a relaxed atmosphere that we had never experienced before in the Bryants' house.

Coincidentally, Mr Bryant was preparing the vegetable garden for the year's produce during Bob's mother's visit and had hired the services of a local ploughman to turn over the large area. To the great excitement of the Londoners, he brought with him a great Shire horse to pull the plough. Just watching the powerful animal slowly and effortlessly trudge up and down was impressive enough, and us children followed its progress fascinated. When the ploughman finished the task, he decided to give us children a treat by offering to give us a ride on the horse's back. Although we were all delighted with the idea at first, when it actually came to being hoisted onto the great horse, we were all, in turn, quite terrified. The problem, of course, for those of small stature, was not just how high off the ground you were, but also that your legs were too short to be able to grip the huge girth of the animal, and stuck out on each side instead. Needless to say, this did nothing to instil confidence or balance and, to the great amusement of the adults, the journey around the garden became a rolling, lurching nightmare.

There were obviously many tears from the girls on the day that Mr Bryant drove Bob and his mother to Crediton to catch the train to London. I couldn't trust myself to speak, as Bob shook my hand, and asked me to, "Watch out for Molly and Joan." He then added, "And no quarry!" It was a sad day and the beginning of sadder times to come.

It seemed that Bob had unintentionally acted as a restraint upon the worst of Mr Bryant's black moods and after his departure a new regime began. The list of tasks and duties became longer and longer. Before we left the house for school, the stone scullery floor had to be swept and then washed, wood had to be chopped and the Austin Seven washed and polished. The car was always kept under cover in the garage overnight, so whatever the weather, this latter chore would always have to be carried out.

It was not unusual for us children to carry out certain tasks on a daily basis and, indeed, Mrs Bryant did have her hands full with cooking, cleaning and washing our clothes. Unfortunately, the adults were seldom happy with our efforts, and scoldings became more frequent. Mr Bryant had a very threatening manner, and we were always in fear of some physical punishment.

In general, we were not beaten, but the girls would dissolve into tears when they were shouted at. One day, when Molly had not carried out some task to the satisfaction of Mrs Bryant, she received a smack on the back of her legs 'to help her on the way to school'. To my amazement, this slap seemed to be the last straw for the girls, and the diminutive Molly calmly informed Mrs Bryant that she would write to her mother if she or her sister were ever smacked again.

In a further act of what I thought was pure folly, the girls began confiding in the teachers at the village school, complaining about the treatment they were receiving and urging me to do likewise. When the old headmaster questioned me about my life with the Bryants, I decided 'least said, soonest mended' and lied, saying everything was fine. My fear of Mr Bryant and possible repercussions forced me to take the coward's path. Although this stance undermined the complaints of the girls, somebody must have thought that all was not right, and one day Molly and Joan were moved to a billet in another village. This time there were no goodbyes; the girls were collected from school and I never saw them again.

When I did eventually pluck up the courage to ask Mrs Bryant about their disappearance, I was told in no uncertain terms that she had asked for them to be moved as they were beyond her control. I was also warned that it would be better for me never to mention them again in that house, and I never did.

★★★★★★

In the spring of 1941 the eyes of many people were constantly turning towards the skies. There was lots of action taking place as the RAF sought to repulse the hated Luftwaffe. The south and east coasts of England witnessed the majority of the action, but sometimes the fight was carried further over the countryside as individual fighter pilots pursued their enemy.

One day at school we were taking our usual morning break in the playgrounds when our attention was drawn to the sound of a 'dogfight' that was taking place in the skies above the village. There were three aircraft circling and firing, but the distance was such that nobody could make out who was who. One thing was certain, however, it was the RAF taking on the enemy, and the sound of the gunfire echoed across the skies. The excited cries of the children brought people from their houses and, as the news spread, the whole village came to a standstill as their eyes watched the drama unfolding above them. The conflict may have taken only a few minutes, but the fight and its finale would last for ever in the memory.

It soon became clear that one aircraft was badly damaged, and smoke could be clearly seen as the stricken fighter began to plunge towards the ground. The cheering of us children and the villagers was spontaneous, and started even before the parachute opened, carrying the airman slowly earthwards. The crashing aircraft and the descending parachutist were now some miles away, and after a little circling two victorious fighters flew off to the accompanying cheers of everyone gathered outside the village school. It was assumed that the departing aircraft were Spitfires or Hurricanes, and several adults were sure that they had identified swastikas on the downed aircraft, which was pretty impressive, considering that nobody there possessed a pair of binoculars or a telescope between them! The sad news eventually filtered through to the village that the aircraft shot down was 'one of ours', and that the pilot, who was Polish, had survived unhurt. The two German aircraft that we had cheered on their way would still have a long and hazardous journey back to occupied Europe, ignorant of the English villagers sending them their best wishes!

★★★★★★

Contained in the occasional letters that I received from my mother was the message that life was still very dangerous in London, and that they were still spending a lot of their evenings in the air raid shelters as the bombing continued. My mother still continued to pose the silly questions that I found impossible to answer, such as: 'Wasn't I lucky to be in Staplelane where I was safely away from harm?' and 'Did I realise how fortunate I was to be staying with the kind Mr and Mrs Bryant?'. Naturally enough I didn't realise anything of the sort. What was apparent, however, was that all my efforts to convey my loneliness and unhappiness were in vain during the present climate at home.

★★★★★★

Slowly the weeks and months passed and, as they did, life with my temporary guardians became more bearable. I still had the usual duties to perform, but practice made me competent, and even cleaning the car became less of a chore, and more rewarding when occasionally the normally dour Mr Bryant would grudgingly concede that I was doing a tolerable job! In the evenings we would listen to the radio, and laugh together at the antics of the comedians Arthur Askey and Enoch, and all the characters in their favourite programmes, such as

Hippodrome and *ITMA*. The more serious programmes like *In Town Tonight* tended to make me feel homesick with its sound effects of a busy city and its traffic.

The Bryants taught me how to play card games, and I became good enough to make up a four at whist, although I always dreaded partnering Mr Bryant!

★★★★★★

Sometime during the summer of 1942, my mother managed to get away from her job in the factory to make the long-awaited journey to visit me. A younger woman, whose name was Elsie, accompanied her. I knew that Elsie was one of my mother's friends, and that they worked together in the factory, as she was mentioned from time to time in my mother's letters. Elsie turned out be great fun; she was a clever mimic, quite pretty and something of a flirt. She was to prove very popular with Mr Bryant and, during their brief stay, managed to persuade him to accompany them to the local inn. This was much to the disgust of Mrs Bryant, and I was very surprised as I had never known the man to take a drink. It was a different story with my own parents and their friends from their part of London, where there seemed to be a public house on nearly every street corner to accommodate them!

Elsie may have captivated Mr Bryant, but she certainly succeeded in alienating his wife, who later told me quite solemnly that however happy the two ladies and their escort appeared upon their return from the inn, they had shocked the whole village with their singing and laughing!

The visit was over too soon and I naturally hated to see them go. It may have been wishful thinking on my part, but I tried hard to persuade my mother to take me home with her. The best that I was able to achieve, however, was her promise that as soon as the bombing had finished for good I would be sent for. Elsie tried to cheer me up by vowing to come and get me herself when the time was right. This promise was accompanied with a wink in the direction of Mr Bryant, which brought a smile to his face, although I was uncertain whether he was pleased at the thought of my eventual departure, or the possible return of Elsie!

Mrs Bryant made it clear that she was not at all sorry to see the two women depart, and as Mr Bryant drove them into Crediton to catch the London-bound train, she celebrated their leaving by giving the house a thorough clean from top to bottom, as though trying to remove all trace of my mother, and 'that baggage Elsie'. Describing someone as 'a baggage' had me puzzled for many years, but it was eventually explained to me what the expression meant, and by Elsie of all people, who fell about laughing when she discovered the reason behind my question.

Children soon learn when to keep quiet in the presence of adults, and this was one of those times. We had long periods of silence in the house during the day, and at night, after I had been sent to bed, there were the sounds of arguments from downstairs. Invariably followed by the slam of the front door as Mr Bryant left the house, and the distressing sound of Mrs Bryant loudly sobbing as she came up the stairs alone.

★★★★★★

It was towards the end of the summer of 1942 I sat a school examination with children of my own age. I was to learn later that this was a grammar school entrance examination. There seemed to be no special preparation for this test of scholastic ability, and it was probably assumed that six years of schooling was enough in itself. In my case I was woefully unprepared, there had been three different schools in as many years, and the disruption and indifferent teaching had taken its toll. In common with many wartime children I realised later that my failure to pass this important test would have far-reaching consequences in my future life. I failed miserably, of course, and could only wonder at the eventual departure of those successful pupils as they went off to the grandly named Grammar School.

★★★★★★

The weeks and months dragged slowly by, and my mother must have come to dread my letters arriving, for I never failed to tell her how much I wished to come home. I was homesick, lonely and, as a result, usually unhappy. Life with the Bryants was tolerable only providing you remembered your duties, and also kept out of 'his' way as much as possible. It was almost impossible to gauge the sort of mood the man was in, as his temper was as variable as the weather. Having to be constantly on my guard was making me an increasingly wary and nervous child.

Sometimes in her letters to me my mother would enquire whether we were all getting enough to eat. Food, it would appear, was becoming scarce in the capital, but for all his faults, Mr Bryant seemed to be a good provider. He had many contacts, and although the fare was plain, the only time that I ever went hungry was when I was too fussy to eat what was put in front of me. Once a week there was a meal of fish that was so salty that even the smell of it was enough to make me retch. This mess would be pushed around the plate until I was able to surreptitiously manoeuvre it into my handkerchief for later disposal!

★★★★★★

By 1943 my constant pleading to be brought home, plus a lull in the bombing of London, eventually brought about a change of heart, and one day to my delight I was told by Mrs Bryant that she had received a letter from my mother informing her of the decision to bring me home. To the best of my knowledge, Mr Bryant was never told that I was about to leave them and return home, and although I could hardly contain my excitement, I took Mrs Bryant's advice, and kept the good news to myself for the time being.

Because my mother was unable to come herself she had asked my brother to collect me. John, who was eight years older than me, had been badly hurt in an accident when he was just seven years old. Slipping down between the platform and a moving train at Kings Cross Railway Station had resulted in the loss of a leg just below the knee joint. It was a terrible accident, and a traumatic time not only for John, but also for our elder brother Bill, who had been charged with his care that day. John was now serving in the Civil Defence, and acted as a messenger during the Blitz, which made our mother very proud.

It was a strange departure, John arrived one Saturday morning, his young brother's few possessions were packed, and we were off within the hour. There had been no time to say goodbye to school friends, or to the vicar and his wife who had shown me much kindness. There was just a pat on the head from Mrs Bryant (her husband was mercifully absent) and we were off in a hire car to Crediton to catch the train to London for the long-awaited journey home. John managed to take the edge off of my excitement, however, by constantly telling me what a nuisance I had made of myself, how ungrateful I was, and that when we eventually did get home to keep out of his way! I soon realised that what was really irking John was the fact that he would no longer have the second bedroom to himself. During my absence John had enjoyed a degree of privacy that had been previously very rare in the two-bedroom council flat that was our home.

★★★★★★

I then spent the rest of 1943 happily attending my old primary school, delighted to meet up again with so many of my old friends. Together we spent most of our spare time clambering through the rubble of bombsites, deserted factories and railway sidings; it was bliss. When money was available we went to the 'pictures', and sometimes we even went when we had no money; it was called 'bunking in'! There was a wide choice of cinemas in our part of Islington, starting at Highbury Corner and following Holloway Road to Nags Head, there were five cinemas, and in nearby Caledonian Road and Finsbury Park there were three more. So plenty of choice there!

There were still occasional air raids, and scarcely a night passed that the sirens didn't go off, but the serious bombing seemed to have finished. I soon discovered that my mother had been right about one thing in her letters to me, there certainly was a shortage of food in London. Everything seemed to be rationed or 'under the counter'. During the summer I did miss the fruit that was readily available in Devonshire, and having to actually pay for apples came really hard. My father was still working on the railway, my mother in the factory, and John made his contribution, but money was always scarce. They were not exactly back to the 'cracked eggs and broken biscuit days', but just before payday every week we would be reduced to very plain food, and little of it. On the credit side, at least I was happy now, and once again looking forward to Christmas in my own home, convinced that my days as an evacuee were over for good.

Chapter Three

Flying Bombs & Cornwall.

The excitement and terror of heavy bombing raids resumed early in 1944. We started using the next door flat that had been converted into an air raid shelter, but never until the sirens went and the bombing began. Many of our neighbours started moving into the shelter at night even before the sirens had sounded, which meant that it could be rather crowded by the time my mother and I ran in. But there was always room for two 'little uns', and amazingly still plenty of laughter in spite of the dangers overhead.

It was early in the summer of 1944 that the doodlebugs began making life a misery for some unlucky souls. The appearance of these flying bombs was almost laughable compared to the sleek fighters that were ruling the skies at the time. The stunted bodies and equally short wing span of these pilot-less machines became a familiar sight over the South of England and its cities. We also became used to the sound of their deadly drone, and the silence when the engine cut out, for it was then that the machine plummeted to earth where the impact of its one ton of explosives caused such devastation. From the streets, and sometimes from the tops of blocks of flats, us Londoners watched and listened to their flight with curiosity, waiting for the indiscriminate conclusion.

One day, I was returning home from school with a friend when we were alerted to the sound of one of these 'buzz bombs'. It was quite low, and it was travelling down Hornsey Road in the direction of our homes. When the explosion eventually came we discovered that the flying bomb had fallen upon Highbury Corner, causing many deaths at what was a busy junction.

At about this time, the much larger rockets, or V2s as they were known, also began to fall on London, causing some panic, and another mass evacuation of women and children began. And much to my disgust and protests I was sent to join this exodus.

It was June or maybe July of 1944 that I once more became an evacuee. I found myself again travelling to an unknown destination far from London. Almost five years had passed since I had been first evacuated as an eight-year-old, and my experiences had made me a resilient survivor.

It turned out that the train we were travelling on was heading west, this time to Cornwall. My eventual destination, via Truro and St Austell, was the small fishing village of Portloe. Another village hall, and another selection process, but this time I was taken home by one of the fishermen's wives as a companion for her son. His name was Frank, and although a couple of years younger than me, he was a good two inches taller. Frank had been impressed with me and my strange accent, which would have been a mixture of country and cockney, and he had persuaded his mother to take me on. This I was to discover would be one of the nicest things to happen to me during my years as an evacuee.

Mrs Trevarton, or Aunt Cissie as I would come to know her, was a local farmer's daughter, and her husband was a fisherman with his own small boat. Mr and Mrs Trevarton had two children, Frank, and an older daughter Florence. Some weeks before I arrived, Florence had married, and moved with her husband to a hamlet a few miles away. Early in the war, Mr and Mrs Trevarton had taken in two boys from Bristol, which had been quite heavily bombed. They had since returned home, but Aunt Cissie was obviously used to dealing with boys.

Until I arrived at this Cornish village, the nearest that I had been to the sea was Southend, and needless to say this was nothing like it! The men of Portloe eked out a hard and dangerous living from the sea, invariably going out alone in pitifully small boats with their nets and lobster pots.

The family owned a small piece of land just outside the village, where they kept two cows and several chickens. Twice a day, come rain or shine, Aunt Cissie would walk the mile or so to milk the cows, collect the eggs and feed the animals. Fortunately, the walk back, laden with produce, was downhill, and there were a couple of homes on the way down where milk and eggs were invariably sold, making her load lighter.

1945, Aged 14.

During my stay with them, I used to enjoy going to the smallholding with Aunt Cissie, helping in whatever way I could. Until this time my knowledge of animals had been gained at a reasonable distance, but now began a real 'hands on' experience. I was even taught how to milk a cow, but never really mastered the art of squeeze and pull, as the pressure had to be just right!

★★★★★★

My 'foster aunt' was a very easy person to be with, kind and generous, and an excellent cook. Soon after my arrival at their cottage, I was introduced to that gastronomic delight, the Cornish pasty! Mrs Trevarton's pasties were not only the first I had ever tasted, but without argument by far the best that I was ever to sample during my months in Cornwall.

★★★★★★

Life in the fishing village was fascinating, the fishing boats were manhandled down to the sea over wooden runners that were rotated as the boat moved, and winched back up the beach upon their return. There were always plenty of willing hands to help, including the older boys when we were not at school.

★★★★★★

That summer and autumn passed quickly and happily, and the strange environment that I found myself in was full of surprises. The dialect took a little getting used to, as it was much broader than the Devonshire dialect, but I quickly assimilated. The nearest school was in the village of Veryan. This was a little less than two miles from Portloe, but there was a shortcut across fields that made the journey shorter, and I never remembered thinking that the walk was a chore. From the first day I was accompanied by Frank, who seemed to be happy to hear of my adventures. These stories I was always careful to embellish with suitable language, which because of my most recent return to Islington had become a little colourful!

The Trevarton family were Methodists, as were many of the villagers, and I attended Sunday services with the family, and Sunday school with Frank. The services may have been different than those that I had been used to in Devon, as the Methodists were mainly lay preachers, but the message seemed all the same. Mr Trevarton's sister played the organ in the chapel, and I was soon enjoying singing in the choir. Aunt Cissie was also quite musical and would play the piano when she found the time, which in her busy life was not often. But it was in her small parlour that I first heard the classic, *I dreamt I dwelled in marble halls*, a song that remained a musical thread in my life.

★★★★★★

Winter came eventually, and we even had snow, which caused some surprise in the village and much delight amongst the children. Frank and me embarked upon a little free enterprise, offering to clear paths and fronts of houses. All went well with some financial rewards until we happened upon one of the grander houses on the outskirts of the village. In answer to our request, "May we clear your path Miss?" the lady of the house answered, "If it pleases you." The two of us did the job competently and were rewarded with a gracious,

"Thank you," but nothing else, not even a cold mince pie! Needless to say, after that experience we were always careful to negotiate a fee before we did the work!

★★★★★★

Sometime at the beginning of the New Year of 1945 I received the sad news of the death of my father. He had died after a comparatively short illness on New Year's Eve 1944. My mother had written to Mrs Trevarton asking her to break the news to me, and this she did with her customary kindness and sensitivity, although I was to remember most clearly the reaction of Frank to my tears. He laughed, of course, which in retrospect was quite natural coming from an eleven-year-old! Had I been living at home at the time of my father's death the news would not have come as such a shock. One of my vivid recollections of my dad was the persistent cough, accompanied by the inevitable 'hawk' and spit, which in those days was thought of as quite natural.

Like so many of his generation he had fought in the 1914-18 war. A Private in the Royal Berkshire Regiment, he was a holder of the Mons Star, and according to his discharge papers had two wound stripes. The evidence of one of these wounds was the deep scar that he bore in his right cheek. But the real damage was that done to his health and mind during those awful years of trench warfare. As a child I knew nothing of my father's experiences in the mud and carnage of France, but I did remember his fractured French, and in particular his shout of, "*Ferme*z that bleeding *porte*" when one of the family had left the door open for the umpteenth time!

★★★★★★

65

The village seemed to be far removed from the war that was still going on in Europe, but eventually all the talk seemed to be of the success of the Allied invasion, and the eventual surrender of Germany. Looking back, I honestly couldn't remember any outward signs of rejoicing in the village of Portloe, and the only sign of a change was the appearance of some of the young men that were even then returning to their homes after being demobbed from the services. May of 1945, or VE Day, was celebrated in the cities, but I only heard of that when I eventually returned to London and my home sometime in July of 1945.

★★★★★★

At the outbreak of World War II, which was in the month of September 1939, I had been eight years old; now at the end of July 1945 I was celebrating my 14th birthday. Five years and ten months of my childhood had been a roller coaster of experiences in different homes and environments, which would help to prepare me for the life ahead. August would be an exciting month, it would bring VJ Day, the return of my eldest brother Bill from the war, and I would start my first job. Now my childhood was officially over.

B. Drummond.

Evacuees

We filed into
The Village Hall
Still fresh with smells
Of Harvest Festival.

Young labelled urchins
We, with names
And our religions
C of E.

Pale city faces long
In need of sun,
And all in need
Of love, yes everyone.

The village mums
Discriminating they,
Picked out the nicest
Ones to take away.

Whilst we remaining
Said a silent prayer
And stood aloof
As though without a care

If no one wanted us
And if we mope,
They'll send us all
Back home again
Where there is hope.